PIANO SOLO

David Lanz

an english garden

www.davidlanz.com

Management:
W.F. Leopold Management
4425 Riverside Drive, Suite #102
Burbank, CA 91505

SONGS FROM AN ENGLISH GARDEN is available on *NARADA* compact discs and tapes wherever fine music is sold.

friend@narada.com

Photography by Rosanne Olson

ISBN 0-634-00191-4

HAL•LEONARD® CORPORATION
7777 W. BLUEMOUND RD. P.O. BOX 13819 MILWAUKEE, WI 53213

Visit Hal Leonard Online at
www.halleonard.com

Sitting in an English Garden

Composed by DAVID LANZ

Moderately fast

mp

With pedal

8vb

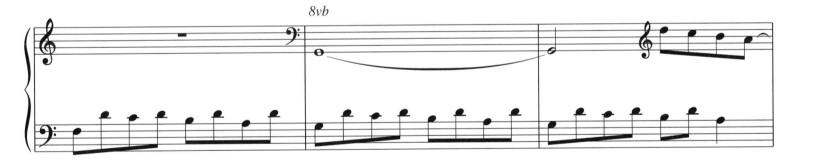

4

As Tears Go By/Ruby Tuesday

Written by MICK JAGGER,
KEITH RICHARDS and ANDREW OLDHAM

Written by MICK JAGGER
and KEITH RICHARDS

Bus Stop

Words and Music by
GRAHAM GOULDMAN

Steadily

(2nd time 8va)

Ferry 'Cross the Mersey

Words and Music by
GERARD MARSDEN

To Coda

28

Tuesday Afternoon
(Forever Afternoon)

Words and Music by
JUSTIN HAYWARD

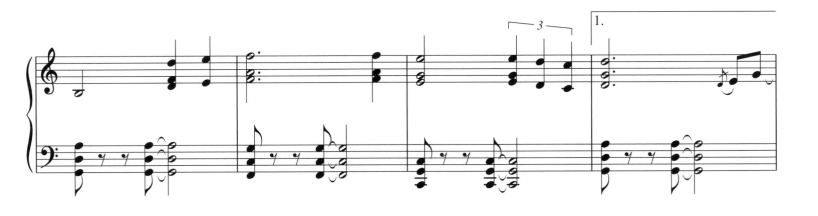

I'll Follow the Sun

Words and Music by JOHN LENNON
and PAUL McCARTNEY

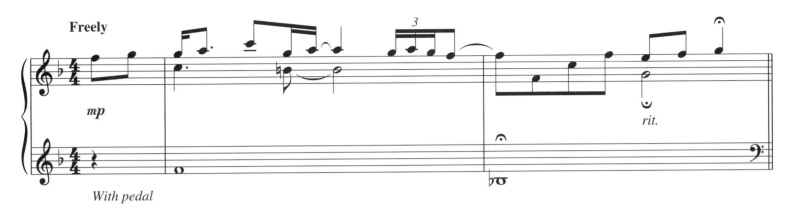

43

Conquistador

Lyric by KEITH REID
Music by GARY BROOKER

loco

8vb

8vb

8vb

8vb

8vb

8vb

8vb

8vb to end

A Summer Song

Words and Music by CLIVE METCALFE,
KEITH NOBLE and DAVID STUART

CODA

cresc.

London Blue

Composed by DAVID LANZ

Moderately

58

Girl

Words and Music by JOHN LENNON
and PAUL McCARTNEY

Moderately fast

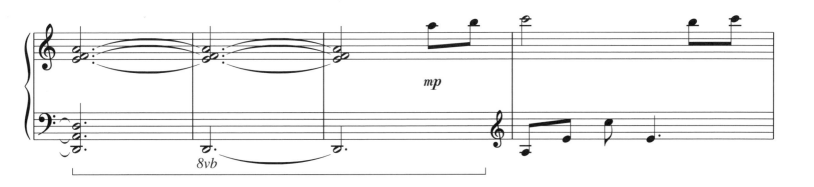

To Coda

Sunny Afternoon

Written by RAY DAVIES

CODA

Strawberry Fields Forever

Words and Music by JOHN LENNON
and PAUL McCARTNEY

Repeat and Fade | **Optional Ending**

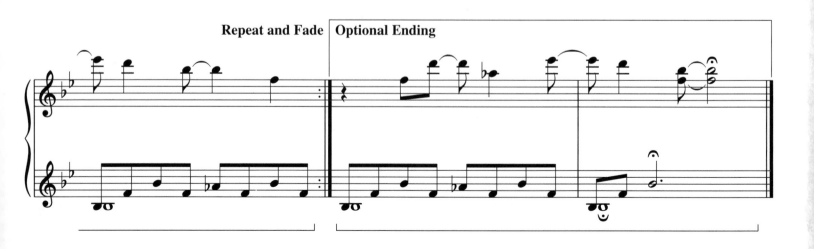